2

EL GRECO

PAINTINGS

Introduction by
Lionello Puppi

Geddes & Grosset

Translated by Christopher Clark
Edited and adapted by Colin Clark

First published 1977
© 1977 Nardini Editore, Centro
Internazionale del Libro SpA, Florence,
Italy
© 1977 Giunti Marzocco SpA, Florence,
Italy
First published in this edition 1990
Published by Geddes & Grosset Ltd,
David Dale House,
New Lanark, Scotland
© Geddes & Grosset Ltd

ISBN 1 85534 004 6

Printed in Yugoslavia

CONTENTS

Page

Introduction   7

Biographical details   21

Geographical index of
paintings   24

Title index of paintings   29

The paintings   33

El Greco

In June 1566, Domenikos Theotocopoulos was still living in Candia (now Iraklion) on the island of Crete (also confusingly called at that time Candia) where he had been born twenty-five years earlier. Here, and in that year, he witnessed a legal document, signing himself 'maistro . . . sgourafos', that is, as a painter. When, not much later, probably in the autumn of the same year, he arrived in Venice, we can assume that he already possessed a solid base of experience and could boast of a good professional reputation. It is not surprising, therefore, that he was soon accepted into the workshop of the elderly Titian who by 1567 was already describing him in a letter to King Philip II of Spain as a 'worthy young . . . pupil'.

It is by paying attention to the sequence of events in the painter's life (some additional information on which has only recently come to light) that we are able to learn about his formative years and the influences, from sources worlds apart, which produced such a unique style of painting in El Greco, the man from Crete.

Although Crete at that time was a possession of the city-state of Venice, late-Byzantine art of the mid-1500s flourished on the island and left its mark on El Greco's visual vocabulary and on his technique. Byzantine forms were frequently used in the decoration of churches and monasteries on the island, but the same could not be said of paintings commissioned by private individuals. These were marked by a tendency to disregard traditional approaches and, through the widespread copying of any available material such as prints or sketches by Caraglio, Bonasone, Parmigianino and even post-Dürer German artists, became more allied with the contemporary figurative works of the West, and especially those of Venice. The fact that artists' workshops on Crete often displayed examples of both Byzantine and European forms, leading to a kind of pictorial bilingualism, is worth bearing in mind. Of more importance, however, are the paintings that El Greco carried out in Western style but that still bear an icon technique and that he produced before he was fully exposed to the actual work being produced in Sicily, Puglia, Dalamatia, and particularly Venice itself. This small but important group of paintings arose out of daily interaction with the Catholic community of Crete to which the Theotocopoulos family belonged.

These pictures throw light on the painter's artistic formation, remembering the ambivalence of the island workshops, and demonstrate the growing preference for Western styles in the work of the young El Greco. His departure for Venice is evidence of his desire for direct contact with European painting, perhaps in order finally to overcome the cold abstraction of the icon technique, although this did produce some excellent results, as in the *View of Mount Sinai* from the Modena altarpiece or *The Adoration of the Magi* (Madrid, Lazaro Galdiano Foundation) which are exquisite prayer-filled works painted in Candia around 1565.

El Greco's journey to Venice was a voyage of research by a young artist whose background and aptitudes carried a peculiarly Byzantine sense of colour, too deeply rooted in him to be entirely removed. Added to this was the huge amount of work he had put into the copying of prints that came mainly from centres where the Mannerist style reigned supreme and that led to his lifelong dislike of naturalistic representation and perspective.

He arrived in Venice anxious to learn, and immediately established a close relationship with the main currents of Venetian painting. From these he was to absorb much technical knowledge without adopting a preference for any particular style, even that of Titian to whom he may have been recommended and with whom he certainly studied. He did, however, attempt to model his work with a more marked sense of mass and to control his illumination in order to reach a coherent balance of space, light and atmosphere, and he developed a sympathy for the work of Jacopo Bassano who, in the seventh decade of the sixteenth century, was producing some of his most amazing night scenes. In fact, *Boy lighting a candle* (Naples) was at one time attributed to Bassano because of its masterly handling of the contrast between the light cast by the burning ember and the lit candle and the darkness beyond that it has failed to penetrate. Also influential was Tintoretto, whose visionary inventiveness was inspiring other young painters during these years.

This conjunction of artists is important because it is questionable whether El

Greco's attention to the works of Tintoretto was not perhaps an appreciation of the formal layouts of his compositions, recalling the complex influences to which he was conditioned. We know that the basis of Tintoretto's art was an enthusiastic adherence to the movement for reform in the Catholic church, which opposed, albeit for only a short time, the repressive authoritarianism of the ecclesiastical hierarchy following the Council of Trent. This adherence to the reform movement is translated into an anxiety about both the choice of subjects for, and the execution of, his paintings, reflecting the anxious moral and intellectual climate of the time. It was a climate similar to the one in which El Greco had grown up, having been born into an Eastern Catholic community in an Orthodox Christian environment. This community, a minority and a segregated one, cultivated a strong and stern feeling for religion in a man of profound spiritual leanings.

His arrival in Rome in 1570 to join, at the

recommendation of the Dalmatian miniaturist Giulio Clovio, the entourage of Alessandro Farnese, Duke of Parma, is inextricably bound up with the presence on the papal throne of Pius V, the stern Dominican who, inspired by a medieval and Biblical vision, was both intransigent and harsh. He was a true pope of the Catholic Reformation and its great aspirations, and as such would have provided a spiritual environment attractive to the devout artist. In addition, the Farnese Palace, with its collections of antiquities and contemporary works of art must have constituted an invaluable source of reference for Theocopoulos to satisfy his need for artistic information. By now called 'Greco' and regarded as 'rare among painters', he found the doors to other circles opened to him. This enabled him to study the best of Mannerism in the works of Perino del Vaga, Venusi, and, finally, Michelangelo, of whose *Last Judgement* in the Sistine Chapel he expressed a harsh opinion, considering it to contain too much nudity. Giulio Mancini, writing about 1619, remembers El Greco in the company of the painters Muziano, Federico Zuccaro, and Sermoneta, and paintings like *Giulio Clovio* (Naples) or the little *Annunciation* (Madrid, Prado) are evidence of his new stylistic temperament.

In all probability coincidentally with the death of Pius V in 1572, the painter returned to Venice for a visit, perhaps via Siena where he would have been fascinated by the highly personal Mannerism of Domenico Beccafumi. It was no longer an unknown though promising young artist who returned to the lagoon (at whose invitation we do not know), but El Greco was certainly driven by a desire to see the development of Titian, of Bassano, and particularly of Tintoretto.

What prompted his move to Spain, which probably took place in 1576, is unknown, but he had met in Rome the Spanish scholar Don Luis de Castilla, who was to become a lifelong friend and whose brother was dean of Toledo Cathedral. He may have heard from him of the opportunities for artists or he may have been attracted by the seriousness of the Spanish approach to religion. In any event, he went to work for King Philip II, joining the ranks of painters busy illustrating the glory of Philip's role as the defender of Christianity and the grandeur of his political designs. After his first attempts, El Greco's fortunes at court rapidly declined, and from the summer of 1577 he took refuge in Toledo, which he was never to leave.

If the homage that he paid to the self-celebrating ambitions of the king consisted of the *Dream of Philip II* (Madrid, Escorial), then we can see the source of their disagreement. In this painting, El Greco reaches a stage of development after which it was no longer possible for him to change as a result of any outside influence. The painting shows the maturing, to the point of tension, of his own spiritual crisis, the onset of which can be glimpsed in his furious experimentation with his original Byzantine sources. His uncompromising religious attitudes were let down by the realities of daily life, and this experience provided a creative springboard, albeit a rigid one, for his painting.

El Greco's almost sudden decision to go and live in Toledo can be explained by several reasons. There were few notable painters working in the city, and there was the presence there of Don Diego de Castilla, the brother of his friend Don Luis and, as dean of the Cathedral, an important figure in church circles. Soon after El Greco's arrival, Don Diego commissioned several paintings from him, including *The disrobing of Christ ('El Espolio')* for the Cathedral, an unusual subject for sixteenth-century painters but one which El Greco was to use again (Munich). Toledo was an ancient city and, as capital of Castille until 1561 ('Gloria de Espana y luz de sus ciudades . . .' according to the song by Cervantes), was a lively intellectual centre, particularly in that 'Siglo de Oro', or Golden Age, of Spanish literature. But perhaps most important of all, Toledo at that time provided a reformist religious climate conducive to El Greco's increasingly visionary approach to art. Two great religious thinkers, St Theresa of Avila and St John of the Cross, were closely connected with the city, and it was the home of the Spanish Inquisition, independent of the Papal Inquisition and an important influence on religious art. Most of El Greco's best work was done in Toledo, the city both inspiring him and softening what might otherwise have been a disconcertingly extreme style of painting. Increasingly in his time there, he moved away from a descriptive style to an expressive and visionary one, concentrating more and more on purely religious subjects, even abandoning the use of human models in favour of wax dolls. Apart from the few portraits that he painted in his later life — including *Rodrigo Vazquez* (Madrid, Prado), the two *Unknowns* (Amiens and Madrid, Prado), and his son, *Jorge Manuel* (Seville, Provincial Museum of Fine Arts) — perhaps the last of his descriptive works is also the best, *The Burial of the Count of Orgaz*, commissioned by the Church of Santo Tomé in Toledo. Here there is a transition from the descriptive and naturalistic human figures of the lower part of the painting, including portraits of notable persons of the city, to the elongated style that El Greco preferred for his religious subjects.

Looking at his religious works, we soon notice his tendency to reduce and simplify his range of symbols. Images become of less significance, serving more and more as the pretext for a free pictorial exercise which derives its sense from the artist's vision. Figures are placed in timeless space, they stretch out, lengthen, move about, they are moulded in colour with a phantom luminosity. Connection with reality, already precarious, becomes weak then almost non-existent. El Greco would accept nothing less than excellence in his metaphor, seeking to unify the apparent world with the world illuminated by the light of the soul. 'Visions, dreams of nature, more than copies of it' is how the art historian Unamuno has described El Greco's paintings of the frantic decade 1580-1590.

It was from the final year of the century, 1599, until the painter's last efforts that his attempts to spiritualize his paintings reached their most amazing heights. The bonds that still remained of his obedience to traditional systems of painting were broken, and the bruised, ghostly figures of his subjects lose all connection with corporality, becoming flashing sparks of flame in a strange spatial dimension. The reign of the spirit world over the fleeting materialism of nature is exulted continually. Again Unamuno points out, 'It is as if the border between dreaming and wakefulness has been obliterated'. The dream is so alive that it becomes the true reality.

This reality El Greco was able to visualize during the long secret hours of silence in his house in Toledo, a house made severe by the almost pauperish sobriety of the furniture and animated only by the closeness of his affectionate son, Jorge Manuel, and his wife, and by the games of his grandson Gabriel, although occasionally it was open to faithful friends.

From Crete, to Venice, to Rome, and finally to Toledo. From the craftsmanship of the late-Byzantine tradition to participation in the triumph of Venetian art, on to the exciting experiences of the international Mannerist movement, El Greco's work is guided throughout by a certain coherence which was destined to lead him to his goal, a formal dimension beyond any comparison. He transferred on to his art his deepest reflections, building up his own language and form, turning his moments of self-awareness into a universal experience as communicable today as when he was painting.

Biographical Details

1541   Born Domenikos Theotocopoulos at Candia (now Iraklion) on the island of Crete (then also called Candia).

1566   June 6 — he signs a legal document in Candia in his capacity as an icon painter.

1568   He is already living in Venice where Titian alludes to him as 'a worthy young . . . pupil'.

1570   He has moved to Rome, where he is mentioned in a letter of November 19 by Giulio Clovio, the miniaturist and illuminator.

1572   El Greco joins the painters' Guild of St Luke in Rome as a miniaturist. He helps in the decoration of a villa

	belonging to the Farnese family. He returns to Venice for a visit.
1576	He visits the Spanish court at Madrid. He paints *Dream of Philip II* for the King, who dislikes it.
1577	By now he is established in Toledo.
1578	His son, Jorge Manuel, is born to his companion, Doña Jeronima de las Cuevas. Jorge Manuel later also becomes a painter.
1582	He paints *The martyrdom of St Maurice and the Theban legion* for Philip II but again his work does not find favour with the king.
1589	He becomes a citizen of Toledo.
1595-1596	There is evidence that he is living in the Escorial, the new palace and monastery built by King Philip II of Spain.
1605	Father Jose de Siguenza refers to him in glowing terms in his *History of the Order of San Jeronimo*.
1611	He is visited in his workshop in Toledo by Francisco Pacheco,

father-in-law of the painter Velaz-
quez and Censor of Paintings to the
Spanish Inquisition. Pacheco gives
an interesting account of El Greco in
his *Art of Painting* that includes El
Greco's comment on Michelangelo
as 'a good man who didn't know
how to paint'.

1614   March 31 — he makes his will.
        April 7 — El Greco dies.

Geographical Index of Paintings

Amiens, France
   Picardy Museum:
   *Portrait of an unknown man
      (possibly Dr Soria de Herrera)* 84-85
Andújar, Spain
   Church of Santa Maria:
   The Agony in the Garden of Olives
      130-131
Barcelona, Spain
   Art Museum of Catalonia:
   Christ carrying the Cross 80
   St Peter and St Paul 81-83
Chicago, USA
   Art Institute:
   Christ in the house of Simon 152-153

Cuenca, Spain

Cathedral:

The Agony in the Garden of Olives
128-129

Illescas, Spain

Hospital of Charity:

The Annunciation 122-123

The coronation of the Virgin 120-121

The Madonna of Charity 118-119

The Nativity 124-125

St Ildefonso 116-117

Madrid, Spain

Lazaro Galdiano Foundation:

The Adoration of the Magi 36-37

Marquésa de Campo Real Collection:

Virgin and Child 132

Marqués de Pidal Collection:

St Francis receiving the stigmata 58-59

Monastery of the Escorial:

*Dream of Philip II (The Adoration of the
Name of Jesus)* 46-49

*The martyrdom of St Maurice and the
Theban legion* 62-65

St Ildefonso 142-143

St Peter 133-135
Prado:
The Adoration of the Shepherds 126
The Annunciation 40-41
The baptism of Christ 92-95
Knight taking an oath 54-55
Pentecost 154-155
Portrait of an unknown gentleman 102
The Resurrection 106-109
Rodrigo Vazquez 74-75
St Andrew and St Francis 68-69
St John the Evangelist 86-87
St Sebastian 148-149
The Trinity 44-45

Modena, Italy
Galleria Estense:
View of Mount Sinai 35

Munich, West Germany
Alte Pinakothek:
The disrobing of Christ ('El Espolio') 60-61

Naples, Italy
Capodimonte Museum:
Boy lighting a candle 42-43

Giulio Clovio 38-39

New York, USA
Metropolitan Museum
The fifth seal of the Apocalypse 140-141
View of Toledo 96-97

Paris, France
Louvre:
Crucifixion with two donors 56-57
St Louis of France 72-73

Rome, Italy
National Gallery (Palazzo Barberini):
The Adoration of the Shepherds 88-91

Seville, Spain
Marqués de Motilla Collection:
Christ on the Cross 70-71
Provincial Museum of Fine Arts:
Jorge Manuel Theotocopoulos 103-105

Toledo, Spain
Cathedral:
The disrobing of Christ ('El Espolio')
     50-53
St Dominic in prayer 114-115
Church of Santo Tomé:
The burial of the Count of Orgaz 76-79

Greco Museum:

Christ or *The Saviour of the World*
144-145

St Bartholomew 146-147

St Bernardino 112-113

View and plan of Toledo 136-139

Hospital of San Juan Bautista de
Afuera:

St Peter in tears 110-111

Hospital Tavera:

St Francis 150-151

Santa Cruz Museum:

The Annunciation 127

Christ saying farewell to his Mother 66-67

The coronation of the Virgin 100-101

St Joseph and the Infant Christ 98-99

Washington DC, USA

National Gallery of Art:

Laocoön 156-159

Title Index of Paintings

Adoration of the Magi, The 36-37

Adoration of the Name of Jesus (Dream of Philip II), The 46-49

Adoration of the Shepherds, The (Madrid) 126

Adoration of the Shepherds, The (Rome) 88-91

Agony in the Garden of Olives, The (Andujar) 130-131

Agony in the Garden of Olives, The (Cuenca) 128-129

Annunciation, The (Illescas) 122-123

Annunciation, The (Madrid) 40-41

Annunciation, The (Toledo) 127

Baptism of Christ, The 92-95

Boy lighting a candle 42-43

Burial of the Count of Orgaz, The 76-79

Christ or *The Saviour of the World* 144-145

Christ carrying the Cross 80

Christ in the house of Simon 152-153

Christ on the Cross 70-71

Christ saying farewell to his Mother 66-67

Coronation of the Virgin, The (Illescas) 120-121

Coronation of the Virgin, The (Toledo) 100-101

Crucifixion with two donors 56-57

Disrobing of Christ ('El Espolio'), The (Munich) 60-61

Disrobing of Christ ('El Espolio'), The (Toledo) 50-53

Dream of Philip II (The Adoration of the Name of Jesus) 46-49

Fifth seal of the Apocalypse, The 140-141

Giulio Clovio 38-39

Jorge Manuel Theotocopoulos 103-105

Knight taking an oath 54-55

Laocoön 156-159

Madonna of Charity, The 118-119

Martyrdom of St Maurice and the Theban legion, The 62-65

Nativity, The 124-125

Pentecost 154-155

Portrait of an unknown gentleman 102

*Portrait of an unknown man
(possibly Dr Soria de Herrera)* 84-85

Resurrection, The 106-109

Rodrigo Vazquez 74-75

St Andrew and St Francis 68-69

St Bartholomew 146-147

St Bernardino 112-113

St Dominic in prayer 114-115

St Francis 150-151

St Francis receiving the stigmata 58-59

St Ildefonso (Illescas) 116-117

St Ildefonso (Madrid, Escorial) 142-143

St John the Evangelist 86-87

St Joseph and the Infant Christ 98-99

St Louis of France 72-73

St Peter 133-135

St Peter and St Paul 81-83

St Peter in tears 110-111

St Sebastian 148-149

Saviour of the World, The (or *Christ*)
144-145

Trinity, The 44-45
View and plan of Toledo 136-139
View of Mount Sinai 35
View of Toledo 96-97
Virgin and Child 132

THE PAINTINGS

View of Mount Sinai from the Modena triptych
(central panel), *c.*1565.
Oil on panel, 37 × 23.8 cm (14$\frac{1}{2}$ × 9$\frac{3}{8}$ in).
Modena, Galleria Estense.

The Adoration of the Magi and detail (opposite), 1565.
Tempera on panel, 45 × 52 cm (17³⁄₄ × 20¹⁄₂ in).
Madrid, Lazaro Galdiano Foundation.

Giulio Clovio and detail (opposite), *c.*1570.
Oil on canvas, 58 × 86 cm (22⁷/₈ × 33⁷/₈ in).
Naples, National Museum (Capodimonte).

The Annunciation and detail (opposite), *c*.1575.
Oil on panel, 26 × 19 cm (9⁷⁄₈ × 7¹⁄₂ in).
Madrid, Prado.

Boy lighting a candle and detail (below),
*c.*1570-1575.
Oil on canvas, 59 × 51 cm (23¼ × 20 in).
Naples, National Museum (Capodimonte).

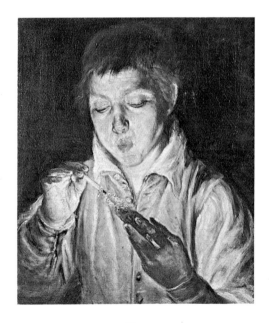

The Trinity and detail (below), 1577-1579.
Oil on canvas, 300 × 118 cm (118¼ × 46⅛ in).
Madrid, Prado.

Dream of Philip II (The Adoration of the Name of Jesus) and details (above and overleaf),
1576-1579.
Oil on canvas, 140 × 111 cm (55¼ × 43¼ in).
Madrid, Escorial (Monastery).

The disrobing of Christ ('El Espolio') and details
(below and overleaf), 1577-1579.
Oil on canvas, 285 × 173 cm (112¼ × 68⅛ in).
Toledo, Sacristy of the Cathedral.

Knight taking an oath and detail (above),
1576-1579.
Oil on canvas, 81 × 66 cm (31⁷/₈ × 26 in).
Madrid, Prado.

Crucifixion with two donors and detail (below),
c.1580.
Oil on canvas, 250 × 180 cm (98³⁄₈ × 70⁷⁄₈ in).
Paris, Louvre.

St Francis receiving the stigmata and detail (below), 1579-1586.
Oil on canvas, 108 × 83 cm (42½ × 32⅝ in).
Madrid, Marqués de Pidal Collection.

The disrobing of Christ ('El Espolio') and detail
(above), 1587-1597.
Oil on canvas, 165 × 99 cm (65 × 39 in).
Munich, Alte Pinaklothek.

The martyrdom of St Maurice and the Theban legion and details (below and overleaf), 1580-1582. Oil on canvas, 448 × 301 cm (176³⁄₈ × 118¹⁄₂ in). Madrid, Escorial (Monastery).

Christ saying farewell to his Mother and detail
(below), 1587-1597.
Oil on canvas, 131 × 83 cm (51⅝ × 32⅝ in).
Toledo, Santa Cruz Museum.

St Andrew and St Francis and detail (above),
1587-1597.
Oil on canvas, 167 × 113 cm (65¾ × 44½ in).
Madrid, Prado.

Christ on the Cross and detail (above), 1585-1590.
Oil on canvas, 178 × 104 cm (70⅛ × 41 in).
Seville, Marqués de Motilla Collection.

St Louis of France and detail (opposite),
1587-1597.
Oil on canvas, 117 × 95 cm
(46⅛ × 37⅜ in).
Paris, Louvre.

Rodrigo Vazquez and detail (above), 1587-1597.
Oil on canvas, 59 × 42 cm (23¼ × 16½ in).
Madrid, Prado.

The burial of the Count of Orgaz and details
(below and overleaf), 1586.
Oil on canvas, 480 × 360 cm (189 × 141¾ in).
Toledo, Church of Santo Tome.

Opposite: *Christ carrying the Cross*
1587-1597.
Oil on canvas, 105 × 67 cm (41⅜ × 26⅜ in).
Barcelona, Art Museum of Catalonia.

Below: *St Peter and St Paul* and detail
(overleaf), 1587-1597.
Oil on canvas, 120 × 92 cm (47¼ × 36¼ in).
Barcelona, Art Museum of Catalonia.

*Portrait of an unknown man
(possibly Dr Soria de Herrera)* and detail
(opposite), 1610-1614.
Oil on canvas, 79 × 64 cm
(31⅛ × 25¼ in).
Amiens, Picardy Museum.

St John the Evangelist (from an *Apostle* series) and detail (above), 1595-1600.
Oil on canvas, 90 × 77 cm (35½ × 30⅜ in).
Madrid, Prado.

The Adoration of the Shepherds and details (below and overleaf), 1597-1600.
Oil on canvas, 111 × 47 cm (43¼ × 18½ in).
Rome, National Gallery (Palazzo Barberini).

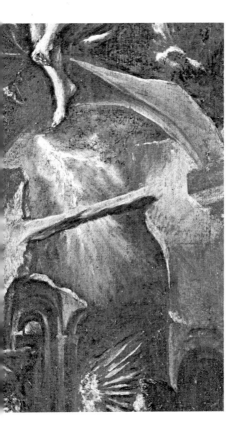

The baptism of Christ and details (below and overleaf), 1597-1600.
Oil on canvas, 350 × 144 cm (137¾ × 56¾ in).
Madrid, Prado.

View of Toledo and detail (above), *c.*1595-1600.
Oil on canvas, 121 × 109 cm (47⅝ × 42⅞ in).
New York, Metropolitan Museum of Art.

St Joseph and the Infant Christ and detail
(above), 1597-1599.
Oil on canvas, 109 × 56 cm
(42⅞ × 22 in).
Toledo, Santa Cruz Museum.

The Coronation of the Virgin and detail (above),
1591-1592.
Oil on canvas, 105 × 80 cm (41³⁄₈ × 31¹⁄₂ in).
Toledo, Santa Cruz Museum.

Portrait of an unknown gentleman 1597-1603.
Oil on canvas, 64 × 51 cm (25¼ × 20 in).
Madrid, Prado.

Jorge Manuel Theotocopoulos and detail
(overleaf), *c.*1603.
Oil on canvas, 81 × 56 cm
(31⁷/₈ × 22 in).
Seville, Provincial Museum of Fine Arts.

The Resurrection and details (below and overleaf),
1603-1607.
Oil on canvas, 275 × 127 cm (108½ × 50 in).
Madrid, Prado.

St Peter in tears and detail (opposite),
1603-1607.
Oil on canvas, 102 × 84 cm
(40⅛ × 33 in).
Toledo, Hospital of San Juan Bautista
de Afuera.

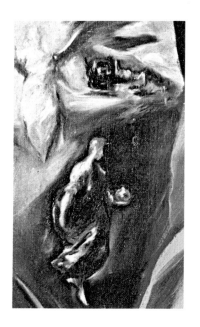

St Bernardino and detail (above), 1603.
Oil on canvas, 269 × 144 cm (105⅞ × 56¾ in).
Toledo, Greco Museum.

St Dominic in prayer and detail
(opposite), 1603-1607.
Oil on canvas, 120 × 88 cm
(47¼ × 34⅝ in).
Toledo, Sacristy of the Cathedral.

St Ildefonso and detail (above), 1603-1605.
Oil on canvas, 187 × 102 cm (73⅝ × 40⅛ in).
Illescas, Hospital of Charity.

The Madonna of Charity and detail (below),
1603-1605.
Oil on canvas, 184 × 124 cm (72½ × 48¾ in).
Illescas, Hospital of Charity.

The Coronation of the Virgin and detail (opposite),
1603-1605.
Oil on canvas, 163 × 220 cm (64¹⁄₈ × 86⁵⁄₈ in).
Illescas, Hospital of Charity.

The Annunciation and detail (opposite), 1603-1605.
Oil on canvas, diameter 128 cm (50³/₈ in).
Illescas, Hospital of Charity.

The Nativity and detail (opposite), 1603-1605.
Oil on canvas, diameter 128 cm (50³⁄₈ in).
Illescas, Hospital of Charity.

The Adoration of the Shepherds 1603-1607.
Oil on canvas, 320 × 180 cm
(126 × 70⅞ in).
Madrid, Prado.

The Annunciation 1604-1607.
Oil on canvas, 109 × 64 cm
(42$^{7}/_{8}$ × 25$^{1}/_{4}$ in).
Toledo, Santa Cruz Museum.

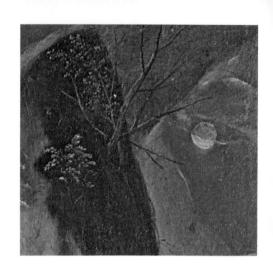

The Agony in the Garden of Olives and detail
(above), 1603-1607.
Oil on canvas 86 × 50 cm (33⅞ × 19⅝ in).
Cuenca, Cathedral.

The Agony in the Garden of Olives and detail
(above), 1603-1607.
Oil on canvas 169 × 112 cm (66½ × 44⅛ in).
Andujar, Church of Santa Maria.

Above: *Virgin and Child* 1608-1614.
Oil on canvas, 90 × 71 cm (35½ × 28 in).
Madrid, Marquésa de Campo Real
Collection.
Opposite: *St Peter* and details
(overleaf), 1603-1607.
Oil on canvas, 207 × 105 cm (81½ × 41⅜ in).
Madrid, Escorial (Monastery).

View and plan of Toledo and details (opposite and overleaf), 1610-1614.
Oil on canvas, 132 × 228 cm (52 × 89¾ in).
Toledo, Greco Museum.

The fifth seal of the Apocalypse and detail (opposite),
1608-1614.
Oil on canvas, 225 × 193 cm (88½ × 76 in).
New York, Metropolitan Museum of Art.

St Ildefonso and detail (above), 1603-1607.
Oil on canvas, 222 × 105 cm (87³/₈ × 41³/₈ in).
Madrid, Escorial (Monastery).

Christ or *The Saviour of the World* (from an
Apostle series), 1608-1614.
Oil on canvas, 97 × 77 cm (38¼ × 30⅜ in).
Toledo, Greco Museum.

St Bartholomew (from an *Apostle* series)
and detail (opposite), 1608-1614.
Oil on canvas, 97 × 77 cm
(38¼ × 30⅜ in).
Toledo, Greco Museum.

St Sebastian and detail (below), 1608-1614.
Oil on canvas, 115 × 85 cm (45½ × 33½ in).
Madrid, Prado.

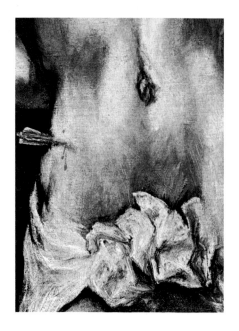

St Francis and detail (opposite),
1610-1614.
Oil on canvas, 90 × 70 cm
(35½ × 27½ in).
Toledo, Hospital Tavera.

Christic in the house of Simon and detail (below),
1608-1614.
Oil on canvas, 143 × 100 cm (56¼ × 39⅜ in).
Chicago, Art Institute.

Pentecost and detail (below), 1603-1607.
Oil on canvas, 275 × 127 cm (108¼ × 50 in).
Madrid, Prado.

Laocoön and details (opposite and overleaf),
1608-1614.
Oil on canvas, 138 × 173 cm (54$\frac{3}{8}$ × 67$\frac{7}{8}$ in).
Washington, National Gallery of Art.